HOW TO WRITE
POEMS

WES MAGEE

QEB Publishing

First published in the United States by
QEB Publishing, Inc.
23062 La Cadena Drive
Laguna Hills, CA 92653

www.qeb-publishing.com

Library of Congress Control Number:
2007000926

ISBN 978-1-59566-344-3

Written by Wes Magee
Designed by Jackie Palmer
Editor Louisa Somerville
Illustrations by Tim Loughead
Consultant Anne Faundez

Publisher Steve Evans
Creative Director Zeta Davies
Senior Editor Hannah Ray

Printed and bound in China

Picture of lion on page 10 reproduced
with permission of James Beattie.

Words in **bold**
are explained
in the glossary
on page 30.

CONTENTS

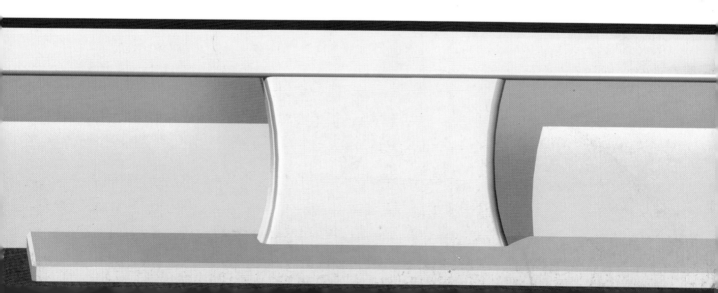

ALL KINDS OF POEMS

People have been writing poems for a very long time. They were written in China 3,000 years ago, for example. Famous poets include playwright William Shakespeare, who wrote poetry in the late 1500s. Roald Dahl's stories are familiar, but he also wrote books of poems, such as *Revolting Rhymes* and *Rhyme Stew*. Today, there are plenty of well-known children's poets, such as Michael Rosen and Jack Prelutsky. Anyone can write a poem...including you!

What makes poetry different?

Poems and stories contain words, and both communicate with the reader. However, there are differences:

• Poems tend to be short and try to convey meaning with just a few words.	• Some stories are short, but many are thousands of words long.
• Poems are sometimes divided up into **verses**.	• Stories have **paragraphs** and **chapters**.
• Poems have a beat, or **rhythm**, and sometimes use **rhyme**.	• Stories don't!
• A poem can make a pattern or shape on the page.	• Stories usually don't.

What are poems about?

A poem can be about anything that you want to express.

- A poem can tell a new story or retell an existing one, such as *Little Red Riding Hood*.
- A poem can be about feelings...what it feels like to score a winning goal, or how you felt when your pet cat died.
- A poem can describe, for example, a sandy beach, autumn leaves falling, or your street covered in snow.
- A poem can be about a person, a creature, or the weather.
- A poem can try to capture a particular moment in words.

Getting ready to write

You'll need a pen or pencil and a notebook. Or perhaps you prefer to work on a computer. Wherever you work, you'll need a quiet place to gather your thoughts.

Different kinds of poems

There are many different **genres** of poetry. Take a look at some of them.

Narrative poem

A long poem that tells a story is called a narrative poem. Famous narrative poems, such as *The Highwayman* by Alfred Noyes, tell stories using rhyme. A ballad is a short narrative poem with a **refrain** at the end of each verse.

Haiku

A traditional Japanese poem that has only three lines and 17 **syllables** is called a haiku.

Sonnet

A sonnet has 14 lines and follows a **rhyme scheme**. For example, in Shakespeare's sonnets, in the first 12 lines, every other line rhymes. The last two lines rhyme with each other.

Limerick

A limerick is a funny, five-line poem. Most limericks are nonsense poems.

Free verse

Most poems have rules, but some poems ignore all the rules. They don't rhyme and they have lines of different lengths. This is called **free verse**.

GETTING IDEAS

Ideas are all around you! An idea for a poem (or even just a **phrase**) can arrive at any time, even in the middle of the night! Your dreams can be a source of ideas. Keep a notebook with you at all times to jot down ideas as they come. Here are some ways to keep the ideas flowing.

Imagination

Use your imagination. Think, for example, of a cottage where no one has lived for 10 years. Ask yourself questions about what's inside the building. If you take yourself from room to room in your mind, your imagination will begin to work.

Feelings

Let your feelings tell you what to write. Something might make you feel sad, happy, annoyed, bored, or worried. Write down your feelings to get you on the road to poetry.

Memories

Think of a place you enjoyed visiting, how you felt on your first day of school, or how you felt when your favorite pet died. Or look at photographs of past events you remember. We all have memories and these can be turned into poems, too.

Senses

Use your sight, hearing, touch, taste, and smell to help you. For example, hold a pebble, a feather, or a leaf in your hand. Make notes about the object's texture, size, weight, and color. This will give you solid material with which to begin a poem. This sort of writing will be mostly descriptive.

Brainstorming

A brainstorming session means writing down everything you can about a particular subject. For instance, you have decided to write a poem about the shore, the playground, or falling snow. Without thinking too deeply, jot down all the words and ideas that immediately come into your head. You can draw upon these notes when you compose a poem.

Automatic writing

Automatic writing means writing without stopping for a little while—maybe two, three, or four minutes. Just write down anything that comes into your head, even if it's the same word over and over again or "I don't know what to write." Whatever you do, don't stop! Perhaps you will end up with seven or eight lines of writing. At first, what you have written may not seem to make any sense, but you may find a phrase, or even just a word, to get you started on a poem.

Idea web

Another way to get ideas flowing is with an idea web. Write a word that represents the subject of your poem in the middle of a piece of paper. Then write down as many words connected to the first word as you can. This may lead you to ideas that you would never have thought of otherwise. For example, in this idea web, the idea of "winter" leads to thoughts of both "cold" and "heat."

presents

baby Jesus

throwing snowballs

building snowman

Christmas

snow

winter

ice cream

ice

cold

bonfires

fireworks explode

heat

woolly scarves

Granny's Knitting

sheep

ACTIVITY

Make an idea web. Draw a circle in the center of a page in your notebook. Write a subject title (such as "robin," "tree," or "my dog") in the circle. Now draw radiating lines (like the spokes on a bicycle wheel). At the end of each line, write down a word or brief note about the subject. Write a poem using some of the ideas from your idea web. You may want to change the subject of the poem to one of the ideas on your idea web's "spokes."

Springboard

Take one of the words or a phrase from your idea web and draw another idea web based on it. Which new directions does it take you? Are there any similarities with your first idea web? Does it give you any useful words for a new poem?

RHYME AND RHYTHM

Many poems rhyme. It's a way of giving a poem structure and rhythm. It can give a poem a musical quality and it makes poetry easier to read aloud, too.

A sequence poem

A rhyming **sequence** poem is a great way to get started with writing poetry. A sequence poem tells you about things in the order in which they happened. In the poem on the right, the days of the week are listed in the correct order, or sequence. Each day, from Monday to Sunday, has a two-line rhyming verse.

The words at the ends of each pair of lines rhyme ("down" and "town," "ash" and "crash," and so on). Lines that rhyme like this are called rhyming couplets.

A WEEK OF WINTER WEATHER

On Monday, icy rain poured down
and flooded drains all over town.

Tuesday's gales bashed elm and ash,
branches fell down with a crash.

On Wednesday, bursts of hail and sleet,
no one walked along our street.

Thursday stood out clear and calm,
the sun was paler than my arm.

Friday's frost that bit your ears
was cold enough to freeze your tears.

Saturday's sky was ghostly gray,
we skated on the lake today.

Christmas Eve was Sunday...and
snow fell like foam across the land.

The week's weather

Mon Dec. 18th	Tues Dec. 19th	Wed Dec. 20th	Thurs Dec. 21st	Fri Dec. 22nd	Sat Dec. 23rd	Sun Dec. 24th

ACTIVITY

Try writing a similar poem about a week of summer weather. First, write down all the words you can think of to describe different kinds of summer weather. For example:

- sunshine
- hot
- cool breeze
- thunder

Choose seven of the different kinds of summer weather words you wrote down, one for each day of the week.

Begin each verse with "On"

The first verse could begin something like this:

On Monday, sunshine in cloudless blue skies

To complete the first rhyming couplet, write down words that rhyme with "skies," such as "sighs," "lies," "eyes," "pies."

By **drafting** and redrafting the verse, you could end up with something like this:

On Monday, sun in cloudless skies,

I'm wearing shades to shield my eyes.

Springboard

Try writing a sequence poem based on one of the following themes:

- the seasons
- the months of the year
- numbers from one to ten

Rhyming Dictionary

Tip

A rhyming dictionary is helpful if you are stuck for a rhyme.

When you have finished, read the verse aloud. Does it have rhythm? Does it make sense? Follow the same pattern and work your way through the rest of the sequence, from Monday to Sunday.

USING METAPHOR AND SIMILE

When you are writing poetry it can be very effective to describe something as if it were something else—something similar. This is called a **metaphor**. Metaphors can create a picture in words—a "word picture." For example, "the wind is a roaring lion" is a metaphor. The poet imagines that the wind is a roaring lion. He creates a picture of a roaring lion in our heads. In the poem below, each verse is a metaphor for the sun.

The Sun is an orange dinghy
sailing across a calm sea.

It is a gold coin
dropped down a drain in Heaven.

The Sun is a yellow beach ball
kicked high into the summer sky.

It is a red thumbprint
on a sheet of pale, blue paper.

The Sun is a milk bottle's gold top
floating in a puddle.

*In this poem, the second line of each verse is **indented**.*

Springboard

Look at trees or at pictures of trees in books. Write a simple metaphor poem about trees. Keep the lines short.

Trees are gigantic, gnarled hands.
Trees are huge mushrooms.
Trees are brains on spine stalks.
Trees are...
Trees are...

Write a poem about the Moon using metaphor. In your notebook, make simple sketches of the Moon. It could be a full circle, a half circle, or a crescent. Now ask yourself, what does the Moon remind you of?

A banana?
A ping-pong ball?
A round cheese?
A silver brooch?
A sad face?
A smile?

List as many as you can.

Select from your list to compose verse 1. You could begin like this:

The Moon is a silver brooch

So far, so good. Can you "extend" (continue) the metaphor? Remember, the Moon's background is the night sky.

Verse 1 could now develop like this:

The Moon is a silver brooch
on an ink black, velvet gown

The "ink black, velvet gown" is a metaphor for the night sky.

Can you compose another verse—or even finish the poem?

Simile

Similes are similar to metaphors. They compare two things to make a word picture, using the word "as" or "like." "My love is like a red, red rose" and "as strong as an ox" are two well-known similes.

ACTIVITY

Write a poem about feelings using similes. Write down some word pictures to describe how you feel about the things below.

Homework is like...
(a swirling, black hole with no end in sight?).

Sunday is like...
(being free as a bird gliding high above the ocean?).

and then...

My computer is like...
Feeling sad is like...
Having no pocket money is like...
Swimming in the pool is like...
The number 8 looks like...
The stars in the night sky are like...

Springboard

Write a poem using similes that contain the word "as." Well-known ones include "as good as gold" and "as white as a sheet." Can you invent some new ones?

HAVING A LAUGH

Not all poetry is serious! Poems that make you laugh are fun to write. However, something that sounds funny in your head may not be so amusing when it's written down. When you've composed a funny poem, it's important to read it aloud to see if it makes not only you laugh, but your friends and family, too.

Here lies
Acker Abercrombie,
crazy name,
crazy zombie.
Slightly scary,
rather rude,
he walks at midnig
in the nude.

Limericks

Limericks are humorous poems. They have their own rules.

A limerick has five lines.

There was a young lady from Deal
Who threw food around at each meal.
   With manners so bad
   She angered her Dad
And made her poor Mom shout and squeal.

Lines 1, 2, and 5 rhyme. These lines have eight syllables.

The shorter lines (lines 3 and 4) rhyme with each other. These lines have five syllables.

ACTIVITY

See if you can write a limerick. Begin with an eight-syllable line, such as:
"There once was a girl with red eyes..."

Springboard

Here is the last line (line 5) of a limerick. Can you make up the previous four lines?

Then slipped and fell down the drain.

Epitaphs

An epitaph is a short verse carved on a headstone in memory of a person who has died. It usually says something about the dead person's character, habits, or how they died. Epitaphs are usually serious; however, they can also be humorous.

Read the epitaph to the left and note the use of **alliteration** (words beginning with the same initial consonant sound). Also look at the pattern of each verse. By reading the epitaph aloud you will be able to "hear" the rhymes properly.

ACTIVITY

Write a four-line, rhyming epitaph for one (or more) of the following:

Dracula
A grizzly bear
Sleeping Beauty
Bucktooth Bill
Monica Moody of Monterey

ACTIVITY

Write a clerihew about yourself. Begin by writing your name. That's line 1 finished! Easy! Make a list of words that rhyme with your name. Think of something to say about yourself and write line 2. Now write lines 3 and 4.

Clerihew

In the 1800s, an English novelist named Edmund Clerihew Bentley invented a new kind of poem. It was a funny, four-line, rhyming poem about a person. The rules for a clerihew are simple.

The first line is the person's name.

→ Mrs. Cynthia Splat
→ owned a black and white cat.
→ They flew through the air
→ on a jet-propelled chair!

There are four lines consisting of two rhyming couplets.

The other lines can be any length.

The funnier and sillier the poem, the better.

TIP

If it's hard to find a rhyme for your last name, find one for your first or middle name—or for your nickname, if you have one.

SNAPSHOT POEMS

You can create a poem by using your eyes as a camera. Look closely at something, such as a wooden bench in the school playground, or a picture of an animal in a book—and take a snapshot with your eyes! Write down what you see.

A good way to turn your snapshot into poetry is to write a haiku. Haiku poems are snapshots and are very short.

A haiku poem has rules:

- It has three lines.
- Line 1 has five syllables.
- Line 2 has seven syllables.
- Line 3 has five syllables.
- It doesn't rhyme!

Here is a haiku poem about a fox:

Slinks to the wood's edge
and, with one paw raised, surveys
the open meadows.

What is a syllable?

A syllable is a separate sound (or part) within a word.

"Butterfly" has three syllables (or sounds): "but-ter-fly."

"Cat" has one syllable.

"River" has two syllables: "ri-ver."

Count the syllables in the haiku about the fox. Does it have the five-seven-five pattern of syllables?

Did you know?

Haiku is a Japanese form of poetry. Haikus are sometimes called "one-breath" poems because they are short enough to be spoken between one breath and the next.

Springboard

Write a sequence of five haiku poems about pets. Make a list of pets (such as cat, dog, stick insect, lizard, hamster, pony, goldfish). Select five. Draft your haiku poems. Remember to use your eyes as a camera!

Write your own haiku poems. Remember to use your eyes and write about what you see. Your school classroom would be a good subject. Look around the classroom and then make a list of items and objects that catch your interest. It could include:

a table, the teacher's desk, potted plants, the bookcase, a display of craft models, paintings on the wall, windows, the door.

Choose four or five objects from your list and draft a series of haiku poems. A first draft of "The Teacher's Desk" could look something like this...

Piles of books for grading,
pens crammed in a cup, folded letters from parents,
the blue register, and a mug of cold tea.

By redrafting and carefully counting the syllables,
the final haiku could read...

MY TEACHER'S DESK

Books left for grading,   (five syllables)
pens crammed in a cup, letters,   (seven syllables)
cracked mug of cold tea.   (five syllables)

See if you can complete a sequence of haiku based on other classroom objects.

A MEMORY POEM

Poets often write about things that they remember from the past. Thomas Hood, an English poet who lived in the 1800s, wrote a poem called "I remember". It begins:

> I remember, I remember,
> The house where I was born.
> The little window where the sun
> Came peeping in at morn...

Automatic writing

One way to get ideas for writing a memory poem is to just let your pen run across the page and write down everything you can remember (see page 6). This is known as automatic writing. Authors often do this when trying to write down their memories.

Here is a verse from a poem about a child visiting an aunt's house:

Remembering a house

Try some automatic writing. Can you remember a house you visited when you were younger? Perhaps it was your Grandma's house. Perhaps it was an unusual house. What do you remember about it? When you have some ideas down on paper, extract a few to use in your memory poem.

Add a refrain

What was the thing you enjoyed most at the house? (At Aunt Lil's, it was her "delicious doughnuts.") Add your favorite thing to the end of your verse to make it like a **chorus** or refrain. Can you write a second and third verse? Don't forget to repeat the chorus!

AT AUNT LIL'S HOUSE
I remember
going to Aunt Lil's house.
There was my uncle's gold watch,
a blazing fire, fat slices of toast,
her yellow canary, two kittens,
and on the stairs...a ghost,
...and
delicious
doughnuts!

When you write free verse, it gives you the chance to make your poem an interesting shape.

No rhyme this time!

Use rhyme if you wish, or create a free-verse poem with no rhyme. For example:

"Who," questioned my mother,
"helped themselves to the new loaf?"
But my two friends and I
looked at her
and shrugged.

Springboard

What's the very first thing you can remember? Write it down, trying to create the scene...
Where was it?
What happened there?
What did you see or hear?
Was anyone else there?
Was there a particular smell?

See if you can write a free-verse poem about your first memory.

A sense of time

You can use your senses to remember things that have happened in the past. Take yourself back to an event and try to remember the sights, sounds, and smells. Can you remember any tastes or how things felt to the touch?

Tip

Don't worry about spelling, punctuation, or neat handwriting when you are doing automatic writing. Just let your pen write!

ACTIVITY

Try writing a poem based on memories of just one of your senses. For example, what pleasant smells can you remember? List as many smells as you can. Then draft a poem. For example:

The pleasant smell
of dinner cooking in the kitchen
on Christmas morning

The pleasnt smell
of shampoo and bubbles
when I wallow in a hot bath

The pleasant smell of...

A PERSONA POEM

A persona poem is one written in the "voice" of someone (or something) else. The poet writes from the viewpoint of another being. The actual author of the poem below could be anyone—adult, child, boy, or girl—but it is written as if the boy in the poem is speaking. He is telling you his story.

Some of the words rhyme, but not in a regular pattern.

I like Emma
but I don't know
if she likes me.
All the boys
think I'm a fool.

I wait beside the school gate
at half-past three
trying to keep my cool.
Emma walks past
shaking her long hair free,
laughs with her friends,
and drifts off home for tea.

Using imagination

This is a love poem. The boy likes Emma, but she perhaps doesn't even notice him. It is also a persona poem. The author imagines being the boy and writes about what the boy is thinking.

Different rhymes

"I Like Emma" has rhymes. If you read the poem aloud you will hear the rhyming words. The rhymes do not occur regularly, such as in every other line. They jump around, popping up every few lines or so.

Animals and objects

Persona poems can express the imagined thoughts of creatures (a mouse or a shark, for instance). They can also voice the "thoughts" of objects, such as a pebble on the beach, the stars, or a teapot.

Springboard

Write a persona poem that involves awful weather conditions. For example, write about someone lost in a blizzard. Keep the lines short and the feeling tense. Remember to write from the lost person's point of view. Don't use rhymes or verses. Just concentrate on making the poem powerful.

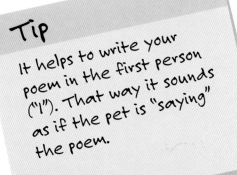

ACTIVITY

Write a persona poem from the viewpoint of a pebble on a beach. Write in the first person ("I") and describe the pebble's experiences. For example, how does it feel to be rolled by the tide, worn smooth by the waves, or thrown into the ocean by a child? An unusual ending might be the pebble being taken home as a souvenir.

Here's an example of a persona poem about a pet cat.

THE CAT'S POEM
Out in the backyard
I find a warm, wind-free spot
and love to curl up and sleep.
I dream about mice...

Redrafting the poem and adding some irregular rhymes improves it.

THE TABBY CAT'S POEM
Out here in the backyard
it's great to find a sheltered spot
where I can curl up in the sun.
This is fun!
Yawn!
I like it when it's hot.
I dream about mice
a lot...

Tip
It helps to write your poem in the first person ("I"). That way it sounds as if the pet is "saying" the poem.

THE SOUNDS OF WORDS

It's important to think about the sounds of the words you choose for your poems because they affect the rhythm and the rhyme (if it is a rhyming poem). The sounds of the words also make a difference because poems are intended for reading aloud.

Snap, crackle, pop!

You can make good use of words that sound like their meanings. This is called **onomatopoeia**. For example, "cuckoo" actually sounds like a cuckoo's call! When you say the word "sizzle" you can almost hear the bacon sizzling in the pan! This poem contains onomatopoeic words. Read the poem aloud. Can you hear them?

THE WATERFALL

Over rugged rocks
    the waterfall tumbles
        and rumbles.

In winter
    it gasps, groans,
        and grumbles.

But in summer it's quiet.
    It just whispers
        and mumbles.

How now brown cow

It can be very effective to group words with similar vowel sounds together. This is called **assonance**. It gives words more emphasis. For example:

A <u>black</u> <u>cat</u> <u>pads</u> across the <u>patio</u>
leaving small paw prints in the snow.

The words "black," "cat," "pads," and "patio" all have the same vowel sound.

Can you spot an example of assonance in line 2?

Springboard

Think about your bedroom late at night. Write a poem about all the sounds you might hear as you lie in bed. There will be sounds in the bedroom itself (radiators gurgling, dresser doors creaking, the comforter rustling), sounds from the rest of the house (the toilet flushing, parents' muffled voices, stairs creaking), and sounds from outside (footsteps clicking on the pavement, a motorcycle roaring, branches tapping at the window, rain pattering).

ACTIVITY

In your notebook, write down as many words as you can for the following:

Words to describe loud noises, such as "bang" or "whack."

Words to describe quiet sounds, such as "creak" or "whisper."

Compose a poem about sounds you hear at school. Write verse 1 about loud noises. Include some of the words from your notebook. For example:

"The screams and squeals of children
in the playground during morning recess"

Write verse 2 about the quiet noises you would hear. For example:

"The ping and drip of wet raincoats
in the damp coatroom on a dull winter's day"

Animal noises

The words we use to describe the sounds animals make are onomatopoeic: the roar of a lion, a dog's bark. Can you add the appropriate "sound" words to this list?

the hiss of a snake
the.......of a cat
the.......of an owl
the.......of a mouse
the.......of a sheep
the.......of a seagull
the.......of a horse
the.......of sparrows

Can you think of appropriate noises for other, more unusual, animals? Be as inventive as you like—the squelch of a squid or the rumble of an ox, for example.

Words, words, words

It can be very effective to include groups of words that begin with the same letter. This is called alliteration (see page 13). Different letter sounds create different effects. For example, soft sounds, such as "w" or "l" can be used to create an atmosphere of gentleness, while hard sounds, such as "p" or "ch" have the opposite effect.

Slowly, the silent snake slips across silver sand.
Clumsy Clive clatters by in a worn-out car.

Tip

Newspaper articles often have alliterative titles to grab the reader's attention. You can do the same by giving your poems snappy, alliterative titles.

"S" creates a sinister atmosphere—and reminds the reader that "s-s-s" is the sound the snake makes.

"Cl" makes a clattering sound—just like the car.

AN IMAGINATIVE POEM

All writers try to use their imagination to invent people, places, and events. You may have never visited an old, deserted house, but it is possible to imagine what it must be like there. This poem imagines and describes the furniture and objects you might find inside an old house.

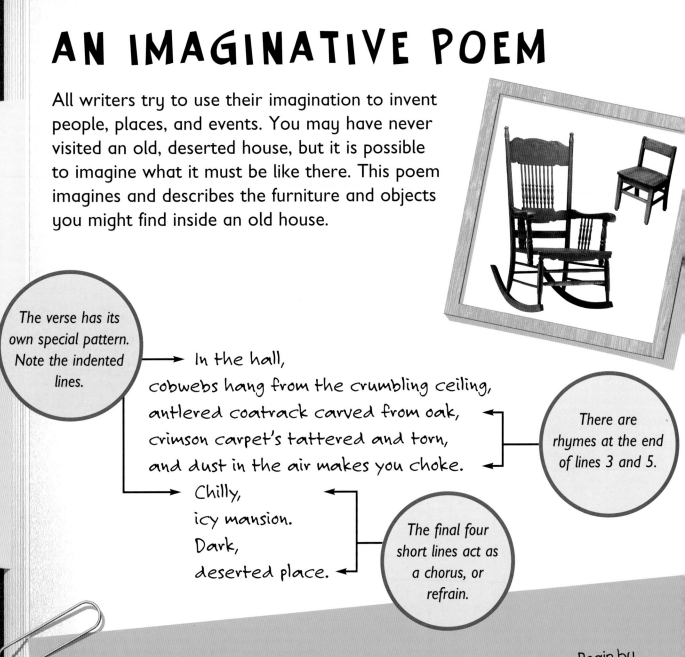

The verse has its own special pattern. Note the indented lines.

In the hall,
cobwebs hang from the crumbling ceiling,
antlered coatrack carved from oak,
crimson carpet's tattered and torn,
and dust in the air makes you choke.
Chilly,
icy mansion.
Dark,
deserted place.

There are rhymes at the end of lines 3 and 5.

The final four short lines act as a chorus, or refrain.

ACTIVITY

Take an imaginary tour of a deserted mansion. List as many rooms as possible that you would find there. Don't forget the attic, the basement, the library, and pantry. Now let your mind "walk" from room to room, imagining all the things you'd see, hear, touch, and smell in the mansion.

Write a verse for the poem. Begin by choosing a room, for example, the kitchen. Ask yourself what's there. Close your eyes and really see that kitchen! Don't forget to add the chorus or refrain at the end of your verse. You could compose a longer poem by using a different room as the subject for each verse.

Stretch your imagination

You can use your imagination to bring to mind things that can't actually be there in front of you. For instance, you could try to imagine what it's like to be on a distant star or to be a creature that lives in an ice cave. Try using your imagination to answer these questions:

• What's behind the curtain on the school stage?

• Who lives inside a hollow tree? (Not an owl or a squirrel!)

• Where do cats go at midnight?

• What happens when the clock strikes 13?

Springboard

It's the end of the Christmas holiday. You show up at the school playground ...a day early! Of course, there are no children to be seen. Try to imagine what it would be like. "Paint" the playground scene in words and don't forget to include the weather, the silence, pieces of litter blowing around, and any creatures you might see (birds, a stray cat). Turn your writing into a free-verse poem.

ACTIVITY

Look closely at a simple, everyday object, such as a pencil. It is straight, thin, and smooth. Now try to imagine it is something else. It could be a rocket traveling to Mars or the fossilized stem of a prehistoric plant. Concentrate hard on that object. Can you imagine other things it could be?

Tip

Avoid repeating words (except in the chorus) to keep your writing fresh and interesting. Use a **thesaurus** to help you find words that have similar meanings. For example, you could say "gloomy" instead of "dark." You can find a thesaurus on the Internet or in book form.

Springboard

It's your eccentric great aunt's birthday party and a lot of relatives have been invited—including you! It's going to be a wild party! Imagine what happens. Describe some of the guests, the games, and the food. Write a three-verse poem, each verse being about a different aspect of the party.

RIDDLES

A riddle is a puzzling poem about a person, animal, or object. The idea is to give clues and the reader has to guess the answer. Riddles are a very old type of poetry. The Anglo-Saxons used to recite them around log fires more than a thousand years ago! Riddles are usually written in the first person, as if the author is speaking to you.

ACTIVITY

Try writing a riddle. Choose a subject from the list below or think of one on your own. It could be a person, an animal, or an object. Make a list of things about your chosen subject. Then use your list to write your clues.

The ocean
A cat
Ripe apples hanging on a tree
A chair
Your favorite cartoon character
Your fingers

What am I?

I am as flat as a football field.
I have legs, but I never walk.
I don't speak, although I can squeak.
People sit around me and eat hot dogs or ice cream but never think of feeding me!
What am I?

Answer: a table!

Tip

If you work on a computer, you can try out many versions of your riddle until you get the right one. Then e-mail it to your friends and see who can figure it out!

Descriptive riddle

Some riddles are more descriptive. They tell you more than just the clues you need to solve them.

I am like an open, yellow eye at night, never blinking, always staring down from the limitless darkness.
And so cold. Oh, I'm so cold!
And lifeless! It's true!

Visitors came to see me, but they didn't stay long before zooming off as fast as they could.
No wonder I look so sad.
Alone and sad in this limitless darkness.

Answer: the moon

Acrostic riddles

An acrostic is a poem in which the first letter of each line forms a word when read vertically. Try composing an acrostic riddle. Spell out the letters of the answer to your riddle down the page, like this:

S
N
A
K
E

Use the initial letters (the acrostic) to write your clues.

Slowly I wriggle through grass.

Now I...

After...

Of course, the answer to the acrostic riddle is easy. It's written down the page! But it is a fun way of writing.

Springboard

Acrostic poems don't have to be riddles. Try writing an acrostic in another poetic form, such as a haiku, or an epitaph—spelling out the name of the subject vertically.

TO RHYME OR NOT TO RHYME?

Your poems don't have to rhyme, but it is easier to give them structure if they do. Rhyming gives poems a "musical" quality. That's why songs contain rhymes! Rhymes also make poems easier to read and to remember, if you want to learn them by heart.

Rhyming patterns

One way to make poems rhyme is to use rhyming couplets (see page 8). The first line rhymes with the second, the third line with the fourth, and so on.

Another kind of rhyme is a triplet. In a triplet there are three rhymes in a three-line verse. This poem is a persona poem about a dog, and is written as a triplet:

My barking drives them up the wall.
I chew the carpet in the hall.
I love to chase a bouncing ball.

Tip

When you write rhyming poetry, keep asking yourself if you have found the right rhyme. Read your poem aloud. Does it sound good or really bad? If it's not right, look for a better rhyme.

ACTIVITY

Write a persona poem in triplets. It could be about a pet, such as a cat or rabbit, or about a person or an object. In your notebook, write down all the things a rabbit, for example, might do.

Sleeps in a straw bed
Nibbles carrots
Eats lettuce and dried food
Hops
Has soft fur
Has long, floppy ears
Lives in a hutch

Think of some one-syllable words that rhyme with a word in your notes. For example, find rhymes for "hops" (slops, stops, pops, tops). Draft the first verse. Can you write another two verses using different word rhymes?

Different patterns

Another rhyme pattern is a four-line verse with the second and fourth lines rhyming. This rhyme pattern is known as ABCB.

Andrew Flag plays football,   (A)
Beth swings from the bars.   (B)
Abbi eats an apple,   (C)
And Steve is seeing stars.   (B)

Try writing a verse with an ABCB pattern. It could be a second verse to the poem above, or use your own ideas.

Non-rhyming verse

A poem that doesn't rhyme and has lines and verses of different lengths is known as free verse (see page 5). Sometimes it is good to write without having to think about rules or restrictions. It's a chance to express your feelings freely or to describe what you see.

A HARD WINTER

Not a twig stirs.
The frostbitten garden
huddles beneath
a heaped blanket of snow.
Pond,
tree,
sky,
and street
are granite with cold.

ACTIVITY

Try your hand at a free-verse poem about a holiday. Draft it in your notebook. Ask yourself these questions:

Where did you go?
What did you see?
What did you like about the place?
Did anything memorable happen?
Did you bring home a souvenir?

Write some lines of poetry. Think about where each line should end. Keep reading your work aloud and listen to the rhythm of the words. This will help you see where to put the line breaks.

Springboard

Try out different rhyme patterns. How about a four-line verse with rhymes in lines 1 and 2 and different rhymes for lines 3 and 4? (AABB) It could even be a five-line verse with rhymes in lines 1, 3, and 5. (ABACA) It's interesting to experiment with rhyme. Try creating your own rhyming patterns.

SUMMING UP

We have learned a great deal about writing poems. Everything from using rhymes (such as couplets and triplets) and different patterns on the page, to sequence poems and metaphor poems (word pictures).

Rules

We discovered that poems have rules. Many rules are there to help the poet. They are useful. However it is possible to break the rules, if you wish. You can create your own free-verse poems, and no one can say to you, "Hey, don't do that!"

Drafting

We also mentioned drafting. It would be wonderful if a poem came out right first time. We'd all like that. Occasionally it happens, but usually the poet needs to make notes (or lists), then write and rewrite (draft). This helps you to finish the poem the right way, to give it polish.

Poems, like songs or hymns, are for saying aloud. If you recite your poem (or poems) to a group or class it helps if you:

- Keep your head up.
- Read slowly and clearly.
- Add expression to your voice.
- Make eye contact with the listeners.
- Add hand actions to emphasize the words.

Keep your poems and make a book of them. Perhaps one day you could be a published poet. You never know!

Presentation

It's good to see a poem finished the right way. This means presenting it neatly and carefully. Think about how your poem will look on the page (or computer screen). This is the poem's pattern. By using a computer you can achieve fantastic layout effects.

Pictures

Illustrations (artwork) always help make a page more attractive. If you don't want to draw, try adding simple designs or borders. Color them carefully. And there's always clip art from your computer, too.

Make notes about everything you might do on a visit to the swimming pool. This is your first draft (see below). Begin to put the notes in the correct order as they happened. For example: Pay at the desk in the entrance. Walk through the revolving doors. Go to the changing rooms... and so on, until you leave the swimming pool. This is the second draft. Write out the sequence, giving it a special pattern (or shape) on the page. This is the third, and final, draft—you have a poem!

Make a list of all the objects and items you might find in an attic. (For example: old books, framed painting, pair of shoes, dolls' house.) Now arrange the list in the shape of a staircase (or ladder) ascending to the attic. You can link the words in the list with words and phrases, such as "and," "as well," or "not forgetting."

First draft

Pay at the desk
Get changed
Get in the pool
Swim for 20 minutes
Get changed again

Second draft

Pay at the desk
Walk through the revolving doors
Go to the changing rooms
Dash barefoot to the pool
Clamp on goggles
Plunge into the warm water
Float on my back
Swim on my front
Swim under the water
Leave the pool
Drip, drip, drip...

Third draft

              Pay at the desk

doors   Walk through the revolving

rooms   Go to the changing

pool   Dash barefoot to the

           Clamp on goggles

water   Plunge into the warm

Float on my back
Swim on my front
Swim under the water
Leave the pool
Drip,
  drip,
    drip...

How many rhyming words can you think of for these words? Make the lists as long as possible.

hair   door   sky   under   tree

Now choose one of your lists as the starting point for a poem.

GLOSSARY

Alliteration the repetition of the same consonant sound at the beginning of several words, within a phrase or sentence

Assonance similar vowel sounds within words

Automatic writing letting the words flow from your pen without stopping

Chapter a major division within a long story or book

Chorus words, or lines, repeated at the end of each verse of a poem or song. Also called a refrain

Drafting rewriting a poem a number of times until it is finished

Free verse poems that ignore the rules and, instead, emphasize expression of feelings or descriptions

Genre a kind of writing, such as poetry or fiction

Indented when words or a line of poetry are set further into the page from the left-hand side than the rest of the words

Metaphor a comparison using a thing to represent something else in order to create a "word picture"

Onomatopoeia the use of words that sound like their meaning

Paragraph a section of a piece of writing, usually starting with an indented line or a line space

Phrase a group of words within a sentence

Refrain another word for "chorus"

Rhyme this occurs when words have the same end sounds

Rhyme scheme the writer's plan for using rhymes in a poem, for example rhyming couplets or ABCB

Rhythm the beat, or "music," in a poem

Sequence a list of things in a certain order

Simile a comparison making use of the words "as" or "like"

Syllable a group of letters that make a separate sound within a word

Thesaurus a gathering together, usually in a book, of words with similar meanings

Verse a section of a poem separated by a line space on the page

INDEX

PARENT AND TEACHER NOTES

- Read poems to the children. This helps to bring poetry alive. Children will enjoy hearing the rhymes and rhythms. Simple counting-out rhymes (such as "One Potato, Two Potato") as well as longer narrative poems (such as "The Listeners" by Walter de la Mare) are always popular. "Let's hear that one again!" is a sure sign that a poem has gone over well!

- Using rhyme when composing isn't easy. The content of a poem can be lost when children concentrate too much on the rhyme required. Children can practice using rhyme by making "rhyme lists" as a separate activity. For instance, encourage them to list as many words as possible that rhyme with "day," "hair," "late," "rat," etc.

- Counting syllables helps create rhythm in a poem (or song). Try a verbal exercise in which you pronounce certain words slowly ("mirror," "certificate," "deer," "vehicle," "ask," "environment") and then ask the children to say how many syllables there are in each word. Alternatively, ask the children to suggest words containing one syllable, two syllables, three syllables, and so on.

- As poems often begin and end on a single page, the children can rewrite their newly composed poems in neat handwriting. This means that the finished page can become a high-quality presentation. Handwriting as art!

- Let the children decorate their poems with patterned borders or pictures. A single picture (or series of pictures) can work well. At other times, the whole page can be covered with background shading. Whatever the type of illustration, the overall effect can be attractive and artistic.

- Word processing helps to give children's poems a "book print" finish. Why not put a number of poems together and create an anthology or collection?

- Children's self-confidence is given a great boost if they have the opportunity to read (or recite) their poems to a group or class. Help the children overcome shyness by demonstrating how they can improve their speaking and performing skills. They should stand still, stand upright, hold their heads up, keep the sheet of paper at chin level, and make eye contact with the audience from time to time.

- If reciting, the children need to speak clearly and use expression. Let them rehearse first. Better still, encourage the children to learn their poem(s) by heart.

- Display the children's poems and add associated objects and materials. For example, summer clothing could go with poems about "Summer Weather" or household objects from the past with "I Remember" poems.